*A gift*

for

_____

from

_____

Children are a *gift* of the LORD;

Babies are a *reward.*

— PSALM 127:3 NCV

# *A*
# DAD'S
## BLESSING

*Given sometimes in Words.*

*Sometimes in Touch.*

*Always by Example*

# JAMES ROBISON

Project Editor: Kathy Baker

Design: Brand Navigation, LLC — Russ McIntosh, DeAnna Pierce, Bill Chiaravalle, www.brandnavigation.com

ISBN-10: 1-4041-0161-6
ISBN-13: 978-1-4041-0161-6

Printed and bound in the United States of America

# Contents

Drivers, truckers, hunters, food handlers,
people who curl your hair —all
receive more preparation, training and
testing than do men who get married
and sire children. To earn a drivers license
you must study the manual,
take a written test, and show
your stuff out on the road.
The man who finds
himself a father receives no
manual and takes no test. But if he
messes up out on the road,
the blame reflects back on him.

— FRANK MINIRTH, et. al., *The Father Book*
(Nashville: Thomas Nelson Publishers, 1992), 15.

# INTRODUCTION

OVER *more* THAN FORTY
YEARS *of* FATHERHOOD,
I HAVE LEARNED *many* THINGS.

One lesson, though, stands out above all the others: The greatest blessing you can give your children is love. This sounds like such an obvious thing to say—of course we should love our children! But the deep, abiding love that follows God's example by giving thoroughly and sacrificially does not come easily.

Colossians 3:17 says, *"And whatever you do, whether in word or deed, do all in the name of the Lord Jesus, giving thanks to God the*

*Father through Him.*" In many ways this verse has become a motto for me, a standard by which I measure my life. So of course, how I love my children must be measured by this standard as well.

Loving your kids sounds easy, but loving them both in words and in deeds can be an entirely different matter. This is where giving your children the greatest blessing gets a little difficult.

It has been said that it is good to learn from your own mistakes but better to learn from someone else's. I offer this small volume as a testimony to God's grace. I hope you will take these lessons and learn from them. As you invest your treasures in your children, remember that you are not alone. Every father, regardless of his specific situation, has difficulties.

As you read, I hope you will ask God to mold you to His standard, to show you how to let His love flow through you to your children, and to let you learn from one another.

"...IT *is good* TO LEARN
FROM YOUR OWN *mistakes*
BUT *better* to LEARN
*from* SOMEONE ELSE'S."

Never forget nine very

important words for any family:

"I love you."

"You are beautiful."

"Please forgive me"

– H. Jackson Brown, Jr.

*"...out of the overflow of his heart*

*his mouth speaks."*

— LUKE 6:45 NIV

Your words are a reflection of what's in your heart,

a picture of who you are. In order to build your

children up, teach them, and encourage them

in righteousness, you must first be a godly man.

Your heart must be a place from which

godly counsel can flow. As you read,

ask God to soften your heart so that you

can hear how He is teaching you.

# "Relationships are More Important than Money"

In *a* culture driven *by* the dollar, relationships often fall *to* the bottom *of* the list *of* priorities; relationships don't hand out salaries.

I had no dad to teach me from the beginning that loving money isn't nearly as important as loving people and that giving is more important than taking.

I did discover these things while I was still a teenager, though, and it has brought great blessing to my life. I have been blessed in marriage for over fifty years now. Betty and I have three children and eleven grandchildren. But we decided when we were teenagers that every time we received a financial increase, we would give to God first.

---

*Honor the LORD with your possessions,*
*And with the firstfruits of all your increase;*
*So your barns will be filled with plenty,*
*And your vats will overflow with new wine.*

PROVERBS 3:9, 10

---

When Betty and I were married, I wasn't farming like the Israelites who first heard the proverb above. But I worked for a paycheck, and every time we received an increase, we gave to God. It became a pattern we have followed since then: *Get an increase, give to God.*

We didn't just give money. We gave our *lives* to people. As we shared what we had (time, energy, advice, and a little bit of money), we experienced *life*. We expressed life, and we touched others' lives.

God says to us, "I'm going to fill up your life. I'm going to meet your needs." And you and I are supposed to keep pouring out what God pours in. <u>Every time there's an increase, why not give to God first?</u>

Taking care of Number One is so important in our culture, and sadly, children pick up on it. It's even come to the point that when people think about doing something for others, sometimes they actually have themselves in mind. You see, people who are focused only on their own needs will think about doing something right and good—but with the hidden motive of getting something in return.

Allowing money to make decisions for your family is dangerous. With every "We can't afford that," parents reinforce the idea that money—not parents—makes decisions. Rather than choosing what is right and trusting God to provide for their families, men subtly teach their children that money, not God, rules their homes.

There's a word for this: selfishness. It is truly an unhappy and unfulfilling way to live.

1 Timothy 6:10 says, *"The love of money is a root of all kinds of evil."* It doesn't say that money is the root of all evil, but the *love* of money is a terrible problem. Selfishness disguised as love drives people to sacrifice other human lives on the altar of personal gain.

Of course, God is not opposed to money. Jesus talked about it often. But His message was: *Don't idolize it; don't worship it; don't let your heart go after it.* That's why God has given us the ability to test our hearts. In Luke 12:34, we're told that where our treasure is, our hearts will be also.

You may say, "I don't have any treasure." Yes, you do. You have the treasure of your time. You have the treasure of your mind. You have talents and abilities. God has given to you something with which you can bless others.

All of these treasures will bless your children.

You are the one who will guide them as they grow, Dad. Starting at birth and progressing through childhood and into the teenage years, you help steer their courses. You take their hands and walk them through elementary school and recitals and ball games. You teach your teens about sexuality, self–awareness, and confidence. Then you prepare them for starting their own families and launching their own careers.

Through it all, I hope you're telling them by your words and your lifestyle: *Relationships are more important than money.*

All three of Betty's and my children were intelligent, capable, and successful as they grew up in our home. Yet in spite of all of their successes and their potential for great earnings, all of them, at one time or another, have said something quite profound and intensely satisfying to my soul: They have each told me they want to pass on what they had growing up. They want homes where love flows to everyone who lives there. They want God to be the center of their lives and relationships. And they want their children to know and love Jesus.

That's what has been most important in their lives to this day. That's what they set their sights on as adults. That's what they all have—loving family relationships.

It's beautiful! And I'm sure you won't be surprised to know: *They have no regrets.*

Betty and I can say, as parents, there may be no greater thrill in life than seeing your children love their children and truly love one another—all because of God's influence. We are seeing this, and it is beautiful to behold. We wish it for everyone.

As you seek to teach your children to have a proper perspective concerning money, I encourage you to pray continually:

*Bless us as we learn submission, dear God.*
*Please help us to remember during this trying time,*
*that nothing we have refused to give away could*
*ever really be ours—You, who promised:*
*"Those who lose their lives for my sake will find them."*

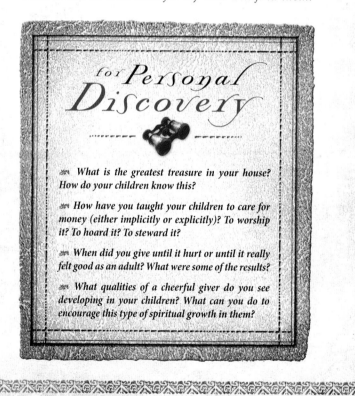

for *Personal* *Discovery*

❧ What is the greatest treasure in your house? How do your children know this?

❧ How have you taught your children to care for money (either implicitly or explicitly)? To worship it? To hoard it? To steward it?

❧ When did you give until it hurt or until it really felt good as an adult? What were some of the results?

❧ What qualities of a cheerful giver do you see developing in your children? What can you do to encourage this type of spiritual growth in them?

TRUTH

Greedy people bring trouble
to their families,
but the person who can't be paid
to do wrong will live.

— PROVERBS 15:27 NCV

# "Speak the Truth in Love"

*Speaking the truth in love,*
*we will in all things grow up into him*
*who is the Head, that is, Christ.*

Ephesians 4:15 NIV

I AM OFTEN TOLD *that* I AM
VERY GOOD *at* SEEING *a* PROBLEM,
CONFRONTING IT, *and*
WORKING *to* SOLVE IT.

Sometimes, however, I don't go about it in a gentle way. I can cut to the root of the matter without much tact. So I had to learn to establish a *genuine concern for individuals* in my heart—which now makes me more effective when I communicate. I know that if a person feels my love for them, they will take my words in the spirit of a caring relationship.

One of the most meaningful things we did with our children while they were growing up was getting together to talk openly and honestly. Betty and I gathered them for times of openly sharing our own strengths and weaknesses. In other words, first we would simply answer this question for ourselves: *What are my strengths? What are my weaknesses?* We would sit there and tell the whole family.

---

"*Nothing* FREES *a* MAN LIKE *the* *truth*."

---

Then we'd move to the next question: *What do I think are the strengths and weaknesses of each member of the family gathered here before me?*

Yes, it was often a bit scary as we listened to each person's perceptions of us. Much good would be confirmed and affirmed. At times there'd be some surprises, too—mostly pleasant ones. But the rule always stayed firmly in place: *Speak the truth in love.*

We would just take in the truth of the others' experiences of us—and we'd attempt to learn and grow from all we received. Nothing frees a man like the truth.

Those family sharing sessions became a wonderful spiritual exercise for all of us. We would not only weep over the kind things the others said about our strengths; we would weep when they pointed out our weaknesses and said, "I want to help." It became a powerful force in bringing us together as a family.

> "*Before* YOU PUT SOMEONE
> *in* THEIR PLACE, PUT *yourself*
> *in* THEIR PLACE."

Creating an environment of honesty in our home taught our children to learn to deal with conflict constructively rather than by bickering or name-calling.

As I have said continually, though, children are always watching. I had to learn to speak the truth in love to Betty also. It wasn't enough to treat my children well, because they also watched how I treated Betty.

When Betty and I needed to discuss a serious subject with each another, I would build her up before we even started a conversation. It encouraged her. She didn't feel as if we were jumping right into problems or negative aspects of our relationship.

Sometimes, people look at communication as being confrontational, negative. Yes, there can be pain, but if your partner is convinced that you love her with your whole heart and she can trust your love, then you are able to open up and communicate. Consider one of the suggestions John Maxwell makes in his book *Winning with People*: "Before you put someone in their place, put yourself in their place."

The truth can be a powerful force in your family, just as deception can powerfully destroy it. Accept nothing less than the truth for your loved ones, and do not let it get lost in the presentation.

## for Personal Discovery

How was telling the truth—or lying—handled in your family?

When you are speaking a difficult truth to your children, how do you show you still love them?

Is there any area in which you need to be perfectly truthful with your children?

By the time a man realizes
that maybe his father was right,
he usually has a son
who thinks he's wrong.

— Charles Wadsworth

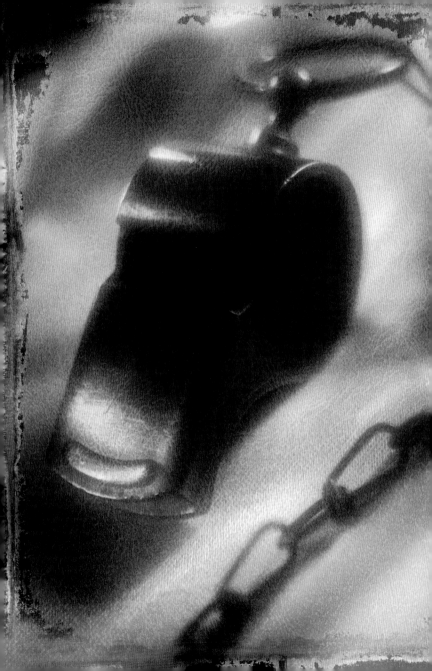

# "I'm Sorry"

*Be kind and compassionate to one another,*
*forgiving each other, just as in Christ God forgave you.*

EPHESIANS 4:32 NIV

## THE BOYS *on* RANDY'S FOOTBALL TEAM SEEMED *to* LIKE ME AND RESPONDED WELL *to* ME.

Of course, everything seems rosier when you are winning, and we were at the top of our game! It was an exciting time.

The trouble was, I got so caught up in the goal of becoming a championship team that I forgot we were supposed to be having fun. As well as the team was performing, I just knew those little fellows could do even better (particularly my own son, who in my mind had all kinds of untapped potential).

In my zeal, I got tough with the boys. I shouted and scolded and criticized, challenging them to push themselves harder and improve their game.

It wasn't a bad strategy, I suppose, if you're a big league coach. But these weren't salty, hardened veterans; they were little boys. On one occasion in particular I knew in my heart that I'd overdone it. I'll never forget the conversation I had with my son Randy that night at home.

"I am *sorry*.
*Will* YOU FORGIVE ME?"

I sat down beside him. "Buddy," I began, "Do you think I might have been, well, a little hard on the boys today?"

He looked up at me and answered gravely, "Perhaps you were, Dad."

Those were his exact words, and they stopped me in my tracks for a moment. The sentence sounded so mature coming from the mouth of a ten–year–old.

"Well," I said, "do you think they understand that I really love them even though I may talk harshly to them?"

"Yes," he replied, "I think they do."

"Do you think maybe I ought to apologize to them for my sharp tone of voice?"

"I think that might be a good idea, Dad."

That was all that was said about it, but in his gentle way, Randy was telling me honestly that I'd gone over the line with my criticism and driving impatience. It meant a lot to him that I was willing to back off and humble myself with an admission of guilt and an apology to the entire team.

As we talk with our children and attempt to impart our wisdom and guidance, it's important that fathers are willing to change as their children grow. You might need to stop and ask: "Have I done something to make you feel this way?" or perhaps say: "I want to change because it will help both of us." This must be your attitude. A basic commitment to humility may sometimes require you to say: "Will you forgive me?"

Just as all men must recognize their sins before God, fathers must acknowledge failures before their children. "I'm sorry. Will you forgive me?" can be the most important words you tell your children when you have been wrong.

Dads, avoid any arrogance. Commit to teaching your children humility by honestly assessing your own actions with your family. As they learn from your example of honest humility, they will begin to walk in the same manner.

Meaningful, happy relationships require regular examination

and adjustment. If you are always right and set in your ways, you close off communication. You're an island unto yourself . . . and you're not very pleasant. When you can step forward and ask for forgiveness, you reconcile an injured relationship and show your children that true strength comes not in *being* right but in *doing* what is right. Go ahead. Try it. You will be amazed at the effect.

## for Personal Discovery

✎ Whether or not your dad is alive, consider: Am I holding any bitterness in my heart toward him? What would it take for me to move closer to forgiveness?

✎ Do your children have anything to hold against you right now?

✎ Yesterday, how would you have responded to a child who thought you were wrong? How will you respond tomorrow?

…husbands should love their wives as they
love their own bodies.
The man who loves his wife
loves himself.

— EPHESIANS 5:28 NCV

# "I Love Your Mom"

*Husbands, love your wives,*
*just as Christ also loved the church*
*and gave Himself for her.*

EPHESIANS 5:25

IT'S NO WONDER *the* EXPERTS SAY
THE BEST THING YOU CAN DO FOR
YOUR KIDS IS *to* LOVE YOUR WIFE.

A child sees her own world is secure and safe when she sees Dad hugging Mom.

It makes me think of a classic film about family relationships, *Wild Strawberries*. In it, an old man, coming to the end of his days, lays down for an afternoon nap. As he relaxes, he recalls scenes from his childhood. One tender memory plays in his mind, over and over again . . .

He is tramping through shadowy woods with his cousin, when he suddenly steps out into a meadow that's blazing with light. And there ahead, surprisingly, he sees his parents sitting together amid the rocks of the seashore. They are shoulder to shoulder, holding their fishing poles, gazing into one another's eyes with smiles that convey perfect contentment. It softens his heart.

> "*Dads*, you HAVE THE *power* TO SHOW YOUR CHILDREN *their* HOME is *safe*, COVERED *in peace*, *and* PROTECTED *by* YOUR LOVE."

In the grip of this cherished memory, all the cares of the old man's life melt away. His successes and failures, his anger and conflicts, all of his long years of struggle and accomplishment come together in that scene of love between Mom and Dad. He is ready to sleep in peace.

What greater peace and security can there be for a child than to grow up hearing and seeing that Dad is deeply in love with Mom?

I wish I had known this! Even now—as a grandfather—I wish I had childhood scenes to recall, scenes that would bring peace to my heart as I lay my head on the pillow each night. But the scenes in my mind would not make a pleasant film. Instead, my earliest memories form a drama with a twisted plot and cast with desperate, needy characters. My alcoholic father, so long absent, came back into my life when I was a teenager.

But he didn't come back for love.

It was not to hold Mom and tell her how wrong he had been. It wasn't to seek her forgiveness, and change his ways, and become a man I could admire. And it certainly wasn't to give me the sense of security and safety I longed for.

Dads, you have the power to show your children their home is safe, covered in peace, and protected by your love. The goal for your marriage should be to have a wife with whom you can totally bare your soul. What you share with your best buddies, you ought to be able to share with your wife. And your wife should be able to share with you, too.

I don't tell my friends anything that I don't tell my wife. She doesn't either. To me, that's great! Why would I be running around with my buddies telling them stuff that I wouldn't tell my wife? If you don't have this open, honest relationship with your wife, it should become an ever–important goal. Diligently and prayerfully pursue it with your whole heart. Your relationship with your wife is not only important for your children, it should be a priority for you!

If peace does not characterize your home today, ask God to strengthen you to do whatever it takes to care for your wife. Begin praying for and seeking a relationship with your spouse in which you can openly share every aspect of your heart and life—yes, even weaknesses and failures. This may take time, but it will prove to be worth the price. God will restore lost time and wounded hearts. And as you allow Him to make changes in your relationship to your wife, watch your whole family. You will be amazed by how they respond as well.

## for Personal Discovery

❧ As a child, through observing Mom and Dad, what did you learn about marriage?

❧ What did your father tell you about marriage? What words or phrases still stick in your mind?

❧ From your adult perspective today, how helpful or damaging were your childhood lessons about marriage?

❧ What do you think your heavenly Father's will is for you, right now, regarding marriage?

A father has enormous power.

About this, he has no choice.

For good or for bad,

by his presence or absence,

action or inaction,

whether abusive or nuturing,

the fact remains: A father is one

of the most powerful beings on the

face of the earth.

— KEN CANFIELD, *The Heart of a Father*
(Chicago: Northfield Publishing, 1996), p. 17.

# I'M SO
# PROUD OF YOU

A dear lady wrote the following letter to my wife and me:

*Dear James & Betty,*

*I watched your program "What a Difference a Daddy Makes." At 78 years old I'm still so sorry that I didn't have a daddy in my life. You'd think the loss would be long forgotten, but there's a hole in my heart that will never be filled.*

*As long I can remember, I was looking for someone to love me and be proud of me. There was a stepfather who ignored me most of the time until I turned 14, when he began to give me attention. Being so naïve, I thought, "Oh, he finally likes me!" I realized in time that it was the wrong kind of attention. It broke my heart.*

*At the age of 16 I ran away with my boyfriend and got married. In the following years, I developed a crush on a married man simply because he was such a wonderful father. I envied my friends who had real fathers. I even came near being raped, simply because I so needed to be loved.*

*Often, in my mind's eye, there's this little girl with arms outstretched. She's just looking for someone to reach down and pick her up and love her. I call her Little Girl Lost. Of course, that was me, until one day at a church altar, the little girl found a real Father who would never leave her or forsake her.*

*My heart aches for the millions of young girls who may not have a good father in their lives. I pray for them every day. Because we all need someone to be proud of us.*

> *God bless you,*
> *"Jane"*

Wanting to be encouraged, wanting approval. No matter the age, everyone longs for it. Often after Betty and I have taped our television program, as we're leaving the studio, I'll look at her and ask, "Did I do all right?"

She usually tells me, "James, you did great."

And I'll say, "Well, honey, you did, too."

Here we are with eleven grandkids, and we're still looking for approval and longing for encouragement.

You have the opportunity to share such words with your children. Even if your children are grown, it's not too late to tell them you are proud of them. Have you grown out of wanting the approval of your parents?

One of the leaders on my staff told me one day, "James, I just wish my dad had told me I did well."

My friend said he was always a straight–A student and an all–district athlete, "But Dad never acknowledged these achievements. I found out later that he would brag to others, but he never said anything directly to me. Because of this, I've developed a perfectionist attitude, and *nothing is ever good enough.*"

Hearing words of affirmation from a father is a privilege nothing else can replace. Even our Heavenly Father expressed His approval of Christ and His work. Imagine how good it must have felt for Christ, amid the disbelief of the crowds, to hear His Father's words: *"You are My Son, whom I love; with you I am well pleased"* (Mark 1:11 NIV).

## for Personal Discovery

✎ *Did you ever hear words of affirmation from your earthly father?*

✎ *What statements—positive or negative—still ring in your mind today? How have they affected you through the years?*

✎ *How are you speaking to your own children? When did you last say: "I'm proud of you"?*

In fatherhood, timing is everything:
knowing when to speak and
when to listen, knowing when to act and
when to be still, knowing when to correct
and when to comfort,
knowing when to lead
and when to follow. Get the timing
right, and your children will
hold you in awe—as will the
rest of the world.

— ROB PARSONS, *The Sixty Second Father*
(Nashville: Broadman & Holman, 1997), p. 10.

# "NEVERTHELESS"

---

*No eye has seen, no ear has heard,*
*no mind has conceived what God has prepared*
*for those who love him.*

1 CORINTHIANS 2:9 NIV

I'D LIKE *to* TELL YOU ONE *of* THE
GREAT STATEMENTS *that* A MAN *of*
GOD ONCE SAID *to* ME.

It was just one word: "Nevertheless." At the time, even he didn't know what it was supposed to mean for me. He said, "I just felt as if the Lord told me to say this word to you: 'nevertheless.'"

He went home and prayed about it and came back and said, "You know, it troubled me all night that I didn't have a clue what it meant. I could only find the word a few times in the Gospels, especially when Jesus said, 'Let this cup pass from Me: nevertheless not as I will, but as You will' (Matthew 26:39).

"What I heard the Lord saying to you, James, is that you are going to go through life with two paths always before you. One way may look better compared to others. But God is saying to you that there are two roads, and never, never, never take the less. Never take the lower. Take the high road. Take more from God's hand."

This simple statement made a great impression on me. God was saying, "Never the less." The "less" is always something that pulls away from Him. The "less" can be the greatest, biggest, most powerful things in this world. But they are always less than the ultimate purpose of God.

---

*Whatever was to my profit I now consider loss for the sake of Christ. What is more, I consider everything a loss compared to the surpassing greatness of knowing Christ Jesus my Lord.*

PHILIPPIANS 3:7, 8 NIV

---

I think everyone gets tempted to sell out for less than God's best. That's why we must teach our sons and daughters to keep God in first place.

When God called me to preach as a teenager, I was full of the energy of a young person. Transformed by God's love, I wanted everyone to know how much He loved them as well.

Then I got very busy, preaching, preaching, preaching . . .

You see, He'd told me He was going to use me and I was going to preach to stadiums full of people. He showed me millions of people and said I was going to preach to them. At the time, I had never even preached in church.

The crowds came, but my love slowly cooled. My priorities gently shifted. It was subtle, but the change was real. Rather than my first love, God began slowly slipping down the list. Ever faithful, though, He called me back and helped me realign my priorities with His.

---

> *"Nevertheless, I have this against you,*
> *that you have left your first love."*
>
> REVELATION 2:4

---

You see, good things—even great things accomplished for God's Kingdom—can take us away from God. That's when we begin settling for the "less" rather than the "more" from His hands. That's when something else slips in and takes God's place in our lives.

Sometimes we don't even realize it.

Men can be distracted from God by work, godly calls to ministry, family activities, and many other things. There's no question those things are good. They are a healthy part of a balanced life. But as the priority in your life, they are less . . . less than our Father's close and constant presence.

My friend, do not choose the less! Not for you and not for your children. Show them by your example how to put God first in their lives.

Every day, you have an opportunity to take the high road, a chance to choose God's best or settle for less. And every day, your children will watch what you do. Make a conscious decision to inspire them to choose godliness, and they will follow you as you follow Christ.

## for Personal Discovery

✎ Did you see evidence of commitment to God in the adults around you as you grew up? What one example stands out?

✎ What do you wish your father had told you about keeping God in "first place"?

✎ What are your children seeing in you, in terms of devotion to God?

What skills are necessary to teach your children these days? To get through life these days, a girl needs training and competence in:

-Automotive maintenance and elementary mechanics
- Small engine and appliance maintenance, minor repair
- Tool use and household repairs, including plumbing
- Elementary carpentry, painting, fix-up
- Cooking and housekeeping
- Childcare and basics of child development
- At least enough sewing to alter and repair garments
- Personal finance and investment
- Personal safety skills and training to use them.

In contrast, what do boys need to cope well?
Exactly that same list. Exactly. Every item on it.

— F R A N K   M I N I R T H , et. al.,
*The Father Book* (Nashville: Thomas Nelson Publishers, 1992), 208

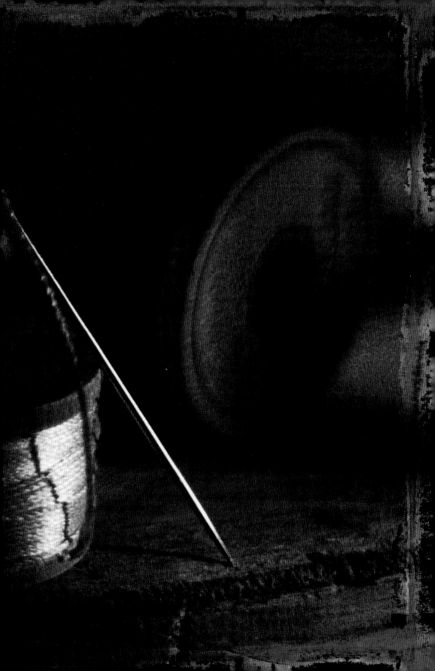

*Dear children, let us not love with words or*

*tongue but with actions and in truth.*

—1 JOHN 3:18 NIV

As your words are a measure of what's in your heart,

your actions give authenticity to your words.

In the end, your actions say more

to your children than your words do.

As you read this book, ask God

to show you any areas where

your words and actions do not agree.

# "I'M HERE FOR YOU"

*No one ever came to the end of his life and said,*
*"I wish I'd spent more time at the office."*

**MANY KIDS SAY *they* WISH**
**THEIR DADS SPENT *more***
**TIME *with* THEM.**

Countless wives say, "I wish my husband spent more time with me." And think of all the grandparents who lament: "Why can't my children give me more time?"

I can relate to all of these needs for time because my own kids would say, especially when I was traveling, that I was gone too much. In fact, I could have lost my whole family because I didn't hear what I'm saying to you right now: Make time—lots of it!—just watching your children, listening to them tell stories, fixing broken toys, doing homework or whatever your children need.

Many years ago, my daughter Rhonda came to Betty with a broken doll. Betty said, "I can't fix it." Rhonda responded: "When Daddy gets home, he can! He can fix anything." I wish that last phrase were as certain as my desire to help.

I don't really recall whether or not I actually fixed Rhonda's doll, but I remember the proud feeling when she came to me with her crisis. She knew that her Daddy would be there for whatever she needed. Rhonda knew she could depend on me to fix the doll, and when she asked, I would be available.

In the midst of a busy life, I was not always available, but by God's grace, no matter how little I was around, they remembered those

> "*When* DADDY GETS HOME, HE CAN!
> HE *can fix* ANYTHING."

words from when they were little: "I'm here for you."

Sometimes life rolls along comfortably with everything falling nicely into place. When you have times of peace, tell your children that no matter what, they can always come to you. Then, when they have a difficulty, they will come to you. Show them by your actions that your words are true. Be available to help even when your daughter's dolls break or your son needs help with his math homework.

When your children need you for seemingly insignificant things, they are simply preparing the waters. I wish the hardest problem I ran across as a father was a broken doll. As my children grew, so did their thoughts, curiosity about the world, and general ability to make trouble.

But because they knew from when they were little that they could come to me with anything, they always did. We were able to deal with their concerns before they became major family issues. No amount of money, pleasure, or time at the office is worth more than that.

No parent wants their children to fail, but wisdom tells you they will fail sometimes. They will miss the mark. And when they do, they must have a safe place to which they can escape. If they cannot come to you when their needs are small, how will they come to you with the truly big problems?

It only takes one rejection for a child to decide never to come to you again. Remember the power of your words to a child in need. Even if your child has been terribly wrong, think about the power of your words as you administer discipline. When I think of teenagers struggling in silence because they are afraid of what their parents might say or how they will respond, I am heartbroken.

Children need to know that they can come to their fathers with any problem. I don't remember why Rhonda's doll was broken, but the point is that she brought it to me. She wasn't afraid of getting in trouble. Then, when Rhonda was much older, she still knew that she could come to me with any problem.

When you feel like you are in over your head, you're not alone. Children are more than any parent can handle. Only God, through the power of His Holy Spirit, can empower you to be a parent.

He can care for your children, and He will give you the strength to do what you never thought possible. He does it with love. We just have to give Him the opportunity.

# for *Personal Discovery*

※ How do you think your children would describe your availability? How would they describe how much you love them? Do you think the two could be connected?

※ In what ways do you let your children know you are available to them? Do you think they recognize this?

※ Are you available for your children? If not, how can you build time into your schedule to put your family first?

Magic is in the air as I walk up the steps to my home and hear my sons inside: "Daddy's home!"

How can children get so excited just because you're there?

We can find it hard to believe that we matter so much to our children simply by being there. It's easier for us to think that we must perform in order to earn our child's love. There's some truth there, but only a bit. *What your children want most is you.*

— PAUL LEWIS, *The Five Key Habits of Smart Dads* (Grand Rapids: Zondervan Publishing House, 1994), p. 14.

# "WHAT'S ON
YOUR MIND?"

---

THERE ARE SO MANY WAYS
*to* FIND OUT WHAT'S *on*
*a* CHILD'S MIND.

*What are you thinking, Son?*
*Anything bothering you at the moment, Honey?*
*How do you feel about . . . ?*
*What's been going on in your life this week?*

Dads who are committed to hearing the hearts of their children
listen closely with their own hearts. Sometimes they simply make

enough room for silence in the relationship, so that a teenager can open up a little without fearing an immediate barrage of advice or criticism. Sometimes it means sharing your own heart first, taking the first step toward deeper communication.

However you do it, you invite a new level of relationship. These times of heart–to–heart conversation uncover layers of hurt, dig up gnarled roots of anger, and remove the dead wood of pride and arrogance.

> " *Be* WILLING *to* *listen*
> *and* *ready* TO WAIT."

Conversation is a special gift because it blends your time and your words. It's different than telling your son he did well in his baseball game (praise) and different from helping your daughter with her math homework (time). It's an occasion to hear what your child thinks about, worries about, or dreams about.

Spending time in conversation shows your child that you want to know what's on his or her heart—what might need healing. You may hear feelings of the moment or longstanding feelings planted and nurtured from early childhood.

Dads must listen closely to all of these thoughts. This is one of the ways to take your child's "pulse." You may hear joy and gratitude.

Or you may hear frustration, disappointment, sadness, or longing. Whatever flows out, keep listening.

Let your children know that if they have ill will toward you, you want to know about it. Where you may have touched a sensitive area, you are more than willing to pull back. Where you have trampled over cherished personal boundaries, you are ready to start over and try again.

To become increasingly vulnerable with one another requires a delicate dance of risk and trust. As each of you reaches out to share, you clear the way for even greater trust. And as trust grows, so this "waltz of relationship" grows into a beautiful display of father–child teamwork.

I wish it had been that way with my dad and me. But I certainly learned why it's so important that we dads listen with a gentle demeanor. Our facial features, body language, and general attentiveness indicate that we're genuinely interested—or *not* interested—in the welfare of the child sitting before us. Do you love her and want this conversation to be positive? Do you want him to go away condemned and torn down? Your demeanor speaks as loudly as your words.

Be willing to listen and ready to wait. Proverbs 18:13 says, *"He who gives an answer before he hears, it is folly and shame to him."*

It takes time and an open mind to give your children—especially teenagers—the opportunity to unload their hearts and bare their true feelings. Allow them to share their concerns uninterrupted.

It may help communication if you have a rule that basically says, "Let's not interrupt. I want to hear you out." Then make it clear by your attention that you want to hear everything your children are trying to say.

After listening to them, let them listen to you with their hearts, too. It may take some work to be able to share your feelings effectively, without shame, and to encourage our children to do so as well. Whether in writing, verbally, or simply as a part of your everyday lifestyle, conversation is truly a special gift to your children. When we are "safe" for them, they will grow to know that they can bare their hearts and souls with us—and with their heavenly Father, too.

If you want to be able to hear a child's heart and be able to express your heart, you might first pray: "God, you are my Father. Help me hear Your heart." God is the ultimate and perfect Father. He is the master communicator and the preeminent listener.

Take time to be quiet and listen to Him.

Then, regardless of how extreme your differences may be, or how painful your past relational difficulties, you can move toward clearer communication with your child. Starting now, you can begin a more loving, enjoyable relationship.

Dad, it starts as you attempt to listen with your whole heart.

## for *Personal* Discovery

※ How well did your parents know you—your true self—as you were growing up?

※ How well do you think you know your child? What practical steps can you take to begin checking your perceptions?

※ How would you rate your willingness to talk with your children versus your willingness to talk with adults?

There is no one else in the
world like your child.
He is literally one of a kind.
His particular combination
of genes has never before
existed and never will exist again.
His label can read,
"An original created by God."

— BEVERLY LAHAYE, *How to Develop Your Child's Temperament*
(Medford, OR: Harvard House Publishers, 1974), p. 52.

# "God Knows the Time"

### Are *you* teaching your child to get away *with* God on *a* regular basis?

One of the things I teach about Jesus' life—and I think everyone ought to hear this—is that He kept pulling away from the urgency of the crowds. He kept getting away and spending time alone with God.

*After when He had sent the multitude away,*
*He went up on the mountain by Himself to pray.*
*Now when evening came, He was alone there.*

MATTHEW 14:23

Many would say this verse means Jesus pulled back to "get His battery charged." I don't think this was the main reason. All power was within Him. Heaven and earth resided in Jesus. He didn't get away merely to receive power. He didn't go to be recharged. So why did He so often seek solitude?

He went simply because He loved His Father. There was intimacy between them, and He enjoyed being with His Father.

I also believe He went to distance Himself from the pressing needs of humanity even though He was the answer to every problem. He wanted to be in the presence of the Father constantly, in contact with His heart and His mind *to know the Father's time* . . . the fullness of time.

Dads need to tell their children about waiting on God's timing. Why? Because no child is born with patience. From birth, they want what they want instantly. In fact, infants probably have the most extreme sense of instant gratification. They believe everything must move according to their own time frames. Children must learn to be patient.

You just can't keep God—or anything that really matters in life—on your own schedule. If you let your schedule run your life, your schedule will ruin your life.

I am amazed by the way Jesus didn't let the needs of humanity dictate His life. He let God dictate the timing, even though it seemed to go against all human logic.

### THIRTY YEARS IN A CARPENTER SHOP?
*What a waste of precious time and energy!*

### MAKING TABLES AND CHAIRS?
*A real messiah would be out with the crowds, healing and saving!*

### DEVELOPING HIS TRADE?
*But what about the needs of the people?*
*Who will care for them?*

It seemed to make no sense for God's Son to stay in the shop. But that doesn't matter. Jesus was continually aware of God's timing, no matter what anyone else thought about how things should go.

This is a hard lesson for children. Because choosing God's timing is in every way against their nature, they must see it modeled in their fathers.

I wish my dad had taught me about God's timing, but instead I learned about it from my heavenly Father. His way of scheduling my days and providing for my purpose in life always amazed me. When Betty and I didn't know where to go next, God opened a door and showed us the way!

People will always try to dictate their own steps, attempt to determine their own courses, or define their own visions. But we must keep getting away with the Father. He truly knows what is best for us.

*For I have come down from heaven not to do My own will,*
*but the will of Him who sent me.*

JOHN 6:38

I recall the days when people told me I was the next Billy Graham. Everybody said, "James is the next world speaker." I heard it every day, and suddenly the measure of my success became what people said.

And then God told me: "You're going to sit down and be more effective than you ever were standing up." I started preaching my crusades sitting on a stool. I didn't really know what God was talking about. When He finally got through to me, He said: "I want you to sit at My feet and listen to My words. That takes time. That means sit down, quit running your legs off. Listen to Me and repeat what I say."

All of this was the beauty of the Father's schedule, the Father's way. The King of the universe refuses to be manipulated.

Our culture will try to manipulate you and your children in all kinds of subtle ways. Your own freely chosen schedule can control you. Then you become a slave to your own life, too busy for your own good. God wants us to learn the role of servant more than the role of speaker.

Dad, God wants to give you freedom. Show your children how God's timing is the best for them by submitting yourself to His authority and living in His wise provision.

## for *Personal Discovery*

🌿 Do you feel like patience is one of your strengths? What did your father teach you about patience?

🌿 How would you describe your relationship with God today? How willing are you to follow His leading and live by His timing?

🌿 What are you conveying to your children about the ways of God? What are the most important things you want to say to them in the years ahead?

🌿 How do your children see God's perfect timing in your life?

I praise you because you made me
in an amazing and wonderful way.
What you have done is wonderful.
I know this very well…
you saw my body as it was formed.
All the days planned for me
were written in your book
before I was one day old.

— PSALM 139:14, 16 NCV

# "My Boundaries Will Protect You"

*There is nothing more influential in a child's life*
*than the moral power of quiet example.*
*For children to take morality seriously,*
*they must see adults take morality seriously.*

WILLIAM J. BENNETT

## TO *a* CHILD, FREEDOM *and* BOUNDARIES SEEM *to* BE AT ODDS.

Rules say, "Don't do this" and "You can't do that." Fortunately, life doesn't work as children think it does. A father's job is to make clear that rules are the structure of a family and to hold his children accountable to them. They are the boundaries within which children can safely learn, play, and grow. Freedom comes only within the safety of these borders.

One of the biggest mistakes people make with God is in thinking that He just laid down the law and walked out of the room. But God says He's giving us discernment and insight—not just about our actions, but about who we are now and about who we are becoming. That's what correction, or discipline, is all about—*becoming* like Christ.

I heard a story once about a little boy who was sent to his parents' bedroom for some "time out." After a few minutes of sitting on the bed, the boy entered the closet and stayed there for a long while. When Dad eventually came in and opened the closet door, the boy looked up and said, "I spit in your shoe, and it's full of spit!"

"What are you doing now?" asked Dad.

"I'm making more spit!"

It's a cute story with a crucial point for us: When we correct our children, we must deal with more than just their *actions*. Their *attitudes* are just as important. A child's attitude shows who that child is becoming.

---

*My son, if you accept my words and store up my commands within you, turning your ear to wisdom*

*and applying your heart to understanding . . . then*
*you will understand the fear of the LORD*
*and find the knowledge of God.*

PROVERBS 2:1, 2, 5 NIV

I believe wisdom is being able to recognize that God's commandments were given as protective boundaries, not prison walls—not to keep us from joy, but to ensure it. It's the vision of the happy child playing in the yard rather than languishing in the street. There will come—and likely there already have been—times when your children rebel against the rules of your home. Stand strong by remembering the purpose of your discipline is to free your children to enjoy life.

"Wisdom" is recognizing that parental correction is for the child's benefit. The goal of discipline is not to break your children under evil requirements of an oppressive parental regime, although most four–year–olds seem to think so. The goal is to build safe practices so your child can grow in an environment of freedom.

If I need to make some corrections, I try to explain *why*. I listen, too, and if I'm mistaken about something, then I can accept that and say, "You know, you're right."

You can make a child brush her teeth, nagging her day after day. But if you help her understand about tooth decay, she may want to do what's best for keeping all of her teeth. She may even ask if she can take a toothbrush to school with her.

One day I asked my grandson, "Alek, what's our rule about the swimming pool?"

He looked up at me with instant recognition. "We don't go near the pool unless Daddy or Grandpa is there!" he recited as if answering an Army drill sergeant. (In fact, he could have added "Sir!" at the beginning and end of that sentence and sounded perfectly in character for a new recruit.)

He was proud to know the rule and to be able to state it perfectly. Apparently, we had trained him well. He knew exactly what his limits were around the pool, and I think it added to his enjoyment.

You see, he knew that we care deeply for his safety. The rule might have seemed—at least at first—like a petty restriction on his pure fun and enjoyment. After all, what little kid doesn't want to run and jump into the water any time the impulse hits? Yet that would pose such danger! As adults, we must set the right limits for our children.

A good father sees his children as *worthy*—worthy of the time that discipline takes, worthy of the energy that teaching requires.

When you get discouraged and feel tempted to let your children have their own way, remember that loving them—your greatest blessing—requires much more than the easiest solution. Remember the goal—a child growing in Christ's likeness—and stand strong.

# for Personal Discovery

※ How were you disciplined in your home growing up? What do you wish had been done differently?

※ What are the most obvious ways in which God has "corrected" you in the past? How did this feel to you?

※ When you consider discipline as being a form of love, what's your immediate reaction? Why?

Fathers, do not make your children angry,
but raise them with the training and
teaching of the Lord.

— EPHESIANS 6:4 NCV

# YOU DON'T HAVE
# TO PERFORM TO
# PLEASE ME

I APPROACHED *the* BLEACHERS *and*
SAW RANDY SITTING *by* HIMSELF
*on* THE BENCH.

It didn't make sense. This was the kid who led the league in batting average and had played so well in the field. And he was starting the all–star game on the bench?

Randy looked unsmilingly over his shoulder as he watched me take my seat in the bleachers. Seeing the expression on his face, I honestly felt as though I could read his mind. He was thinking, "*I know Dad is really disappointed and upset to see me on the bench. Dear God, please don't let him say anything or let it show."*

By the grace of God, that was one of those moments when I got it right. While I was still in my car driving from the airport to the game, I felt strongly impressed that I somehow needed to convey to my son how thoroughly proud I was of him—and that he didn't need to "perform" to get my approval.

I walked over to the fence and leaned over. Randy looked up at me somewhat apprehensively.

"Randy," I said, "I want you to know I am just as proud of you sitting right here on this bench as I would be if you were starting at third base and hitting home runs. There's no way I could ever be more proud of you. You're my son, and you don't have to do anything to please me or to gain my approval. You've got it one hundred percent. I love you, Son."

Tears filled his eyes and he smiled. Somehow I knew I had struck a chord. And with thanks to God in my heart, I knew I had done exactly the right thing.

That was many years ago, and it is still a precious memory for me. I believe it was a crucial day for Randy, too.

As children grow, dads need to say to them: *"Always do your best—and don't be afraid to fail."* I think of the little kid who strikes out and drags his bat back to the dugout. He's going to turn his eyes up to the bleachers to his daddy. Daddy needs to let him know that he's just as proud as he would be if the boy had hit it over the fence. That little boy needs to hear it because he needs to know that his acceptance is not based on his performance. Acceptance is based on relationship: *"I am family, and Daddy is proud of me."*

---

## "*Always* DO YOUR *best* and DON'T BE *afraid to* FAIL."

---

I have struck out in life many times. And when I take that third swing and fan the air, the thing that's so wonderful about God is that He says to me: "I know you tried. We're going to try some more. But if you never hit it where it's supposed to be hit, I'm still proud of you, I still love you, and it's great to know that you're trying to please Me."

I have grandkids now, and when they come to me they're usually saying, "Papaw, let's do this, let's do that!" They come from everywhere like fleas on a dog! But I've got one little grandson who comes to my chair and crawls up in my lap. Often he says, "Hold me."

I just melt.

Then he'll roll his eyes up at me and say, "Papaw, what do *you* want to do?" That's one of the strongest things God ever showed me. I need to go to my heavenly Father and say, "God, what do *You* want to do?" It pleases God greatly when we are as anxious to hear His heart as we are for Him to hear our hearts.

When we do that, we remind ourselves that God is the all–powerful "performer" in our lives. We are not required to achieve any certain status or put on a special show. We simply need to look to God to see what He wants to do next, waiting to see how He will bring us into the picture.

Remember, He is fully able to accomplish His work. His success doesn't depend on our success. He simply calls us to be involved in whatever He intends to do. We can be a part of fulfilling the desires of our Father's heart.

In the same way, your success does not depend on your children's success. Simply invite them into your life no matter what they do or how they perform.

## for Personal Discovery

※ To what extent were you a "performer" as a child? What memories of this come to mind at the moment?

※ How approval–oriented are you today? How do you think your relationship with your father (present or absent) influenced this?

※ What comes to mind when you think about "the grace of God"? Do you believe your heavenly Father approves of you? How do you know?

BLESSINGS

Dreams are more than just idle thoughts
or powerless wishes, for as a father dreams,
so will he teach, encourage, nurture, and guide.
The hopes and dreams a woman
has for herself are often shaped
by those her father has for her.
He can either close windows of
opportunity, or open a world of
possibilities for his little girl.
That's why dreams are important for
daddies and their daughters.
Dreams keep us in tune with the
present while adding hope for the future.

— CARMEN BERRY and LYNN BARRINGTON, *Daddies and Daughters*
(New York: Simon & Schuster, 1998), p. 57.

# THE POWER OF
# A DAD'S BLESSING

*Death and life are in the power of the tongue.*

PROVERBS 18:21

As I think back to the years when my children were growing up, I remember the power my words held in their lives . . . life and death for them. That seems like such a dramatic thing to say, but it's true. My harsh, critical, or angry words crushed their spirits. But my gentle, encouraging words of promise brought life to their hearts.

If I could choose one lesson to drive home to you, I choose this one: The power of a father's blessing is one of the strongest influences in a child's life. After torturous growing–up years, I came to know Christ at the age of fourteen through the love and affection of my foster parents. The shadow of impending failure cast by my past seemed overwhelming, like I could never do any good, but my adoptive parents' words cast a vision of hope I had never dreamed possible.

I love how God has a much different plan for His children than any of us can imagine. When I was eighteen, God called me to preach. Nobody really believed it because I was so shy, which is funny if you know me now. In fact, I don't think I would have believed it if He hadn't spoken to me so clearly. I asked several deacons at my church, and they all thought I had merely overheard God's call to someone else.

But God's words cast a vision of prosperity and productivity much different from some people's dire forecast for my life. Three days after He called me, I preached my first sermon on a flatbed truck at a construction job.

That was the beginning of choosing God's blessing over the predictions of others. The words of promise from my Father drove me to excellence, and I have preached to more than twenty million people in person.

No matter how much you love your children, your words will be a blessing or a curse on their lives. Your words hold a power much greater than anyone else's. Proverbs 18:21 cautions, "Death and life are in the power of the tongue."

In so many ways, this verse is true, even down to training your child in success. You must consciously give your blessing to your children. The words you speak over your children will shape their lives. By specifically lifting up each of my children, I planted life in their hearts. Those seeds of promise are still bearing fruit today. My children are successful in part because their father told them they could be.

Dad, carefully pour your blessings over your children. When they fail, shower them with encouragement. When they are scared, tell them how to be strong. I knew I could be a preacher simply because my heavenly Father said so. Just as God spoke blessing into my life, so your words of blessing will give life to your children.

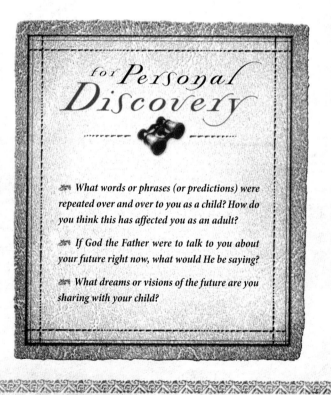

## for Personal Discovery

❧ What words or phrases (or predictions) were repeated over and over to you as a child? How do you think this has affected you as an adult?

❧ If God the Father were to talk to you about your future right now, what would He be saying?

❧ What dreams or visions of the future are you sharing with your child?

In my own childhood and boyhood my father
was the refuge from all the ills of life,
even sharp pain itself.
Therefore I say to the son or daughter who has
no pleasure in the name Father,
"You must interpret the word by
all that you have missed in life.
All that human tenderness
can give or desire in the nearness
and readiness of love, all and
infinitely more must be
true of the perfect Father
—of the maker of fatherhood."

— *The Heart of George MacDonald: A One-Volume Collection of His Most Important Fiction,
Essays, Sermons, Drama, Poetry, Letters* (Wheaton Literary)

# EPILOGUE

We have looked at many aspects of being a father
and come back to one thing:

"Whatever you do in word or deed,
do all in the name of the Lord Jesus,
giving thanks to God the Father through Him"
(Colossians 3:17).

As a father, everything comes back to this.
Whatever you do for your wife,
for your family, for your children . . .
do it all in the name of the Lord Jesus.

It would be a tragedy if my kids grew up knowing only that their dad was a good football player and husband and father. If I expected them to live every minute of their lives the way they have seen me live as they grew up, they would be frustrated and devastated if they ever failed. I want them to know what they didn't see, when I failed miserably and only came out of it by the grace of God . . . I also want them to know of my mistakes because they will make their own, and I don't want them to feel they are the first person in the family to fail . . . .

Most of all, I want them to know that by the grace of God, He brought me through it and out of it, and He can do the same for them.

–MIKE SINGLETARY, *Men's Devotional Bible* (Grand Rapids: Zondervan Publishing House, 1993), p. 475.

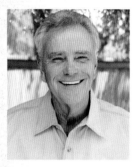

JAMES ROBISON is the founder and president of LIFE Outreach International in Fort Worth, Texas. LIFE Outreach is a Christian organization that offers hope and help to the suffering worldwide through feeding programs, water-well drilling and other acts of compassion. Others have come to know James as one of America's most popular television talk-show hosts. *LIFE TODAY*, which he co-hosts with his wife, Betty, is a ministry of LIFE Outreach and reaches a billion people in the United States, Canada and throughout Europe and Australia. James and Betty are the parents of three children and have eleven grandchildren.

What encouragement might sound like:

-"I know it's going to be hard, but I believe in you."

- "What can I do to help you accomplish
                        your goals this week?"

- "If anyone can make it, you can,
            and I'd like to join you in that goal"

- "Tomorrow's a new day,
        and I'm excited to live it with you."

— DAVID AND TERESA FERGUSON
*More Than Married* (Nashville: J. Countryman, 2000), 85

No one ever came to the

end of his life and said,

"I wish I'd spent

more time at the office."